Defenestration

Indrani Perera

Defenestration

For Jan

Defenestration
ISBN 978 1 876259 17 4
Copyright © text Indrani Perera 1997
Copyright © artwork Jan Easter 1997

First published 1997
Reprinted 2018

Ginninderra Press
PO Box 3461 Port Adelaide 5015
www.ginninderrapress.com.au

First lines

Come boy	7
I was betrayed by a kiss, stolen from time	8
The acrid smell of smoke	9
And I can't imagine	11
I so wanted to believe	12
Weep no more, good lady	13
I can see	14
There's a ghost that wanders through the hallways	15
I'm an impostor	17
I've lost sight of that path	18
It's funny, you know	19
There were no fireworks	20
I will wait for you at the corner store	21
The lock of hair tumbles on to his forehead	22
The jester sits	25
What maketh the man?" the famous man once asked	26
On West 46 and Broadway	31
Revolting, repugnant, repulsive	32
Zombie turned square-eyes	33
As a woman I am privileged	34
Gaunt human skeleton	35
Bloodied hands ripping out	36
Hair flaming amazement	37
Professional women	38
Vitriolic, vicious stream of abuse	39
Fanatical, twisted mind	40
Primitive, rhythmic, orgasmic	41
Yet still I live	42

Come boy
worship at my feet
pay homage to my shrine
and be blessed in my temple

Come boy
kiss my feet
carry my baggage for me
oh, body-slave mine

Come boy
grovel at my feet
abase yourself before me
avert your eyes

Come boy
and be punished for thy crime
wear the stripes of the whip with pride
and never forget the sting of salt in your wounds

I was betrayed by a kiss, stolen from time
when I thought God wasn't looking
caught red-handed, blood on my fingers
from the heart of the sweet, kind
and yet uncaring, inattentive, oblivious man
who was trapping my mind in the mundane
sucking my soul into oblivion, eyes blank
unseeing, unseen, unable to see the world
trapped in this bleak landscape of existence
not living free, soaring, seeking, thirsting for knowledge

Ironic isn't it, that, as I have betrayed my lover
I am in turn betrayed by my lover
perhaps a just punishment for my crime
a crime of trying to cheat good old father time
tick-tick-tocking the days of my life
measuring in cadence the motions, movements, minutiae
of my life, assigning each to its proper place
gently slapping my hand when I try to cheat
or smacking me in the mouth with a dry fish
as the lies lie still on my tongue once more
ending this game of deceit

The acrid smell of smoke
as the match strikes once
against the box
then lights

The indrawn breath
eyes narrowed against the smoke
as the end of the cigarette
glows against the dark of night

The traces of tears on the face
once wet and now dry
as she hardens her heart
against what must come

The expelled breath
as she exhales the smoke
and the poison from her lungs
and stills her beating heart

Lovingly she consumes the cigarette
as her addiction consumes her
always a price to be paid here
and it's a truth her heart knows

And the knowledge hardens
into a kernel to lodge
painfully
somewhere deep in the psyche

Just one more piece of baggage now
just add it to all the others
just carry it around for all your days
the lesson so painfully learned

Slowly, lingering, she takes her last drag
much as a lover would take their last kiss
expels the smoke, slowly, making it last
savouring the damage done, the hurt and the pain

Before crushing it with all the others in the ashtray
ashes now, all of it, of her hopes and dreams
and then, inexorably, the hand reaches for another
and she begins again, her destiny until her lesson is learnt

And I can't imagine
that I let you further through the door
than any other salesman who's come calling before
only to find that you were selling the same as them
lies, deceit, heartache and pain

I so wanted to believe
to believe in the words
from, not stolen by, a poet
to believe in the dream

And I really wanted to believe
to believe that this time
it would be right
and the words would be true

But now I believe
that the only thing
I can believe in
is pain

And I believe
that this pain
will make me stronger
just add it to all the others

But when will it end?
Where's the pot of gold, the pay-off?
How strong do I have to be?

Weep no more, good lady
throw off the clothes of mourning
leave them in a cupboard
to become moth-eaten and covered in dust
to be found a lifetime later
by another to wear

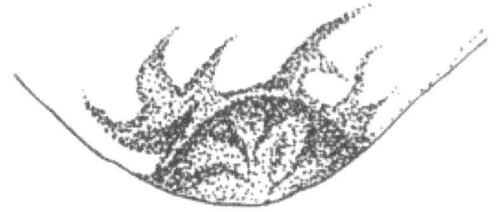

I can see
from the quizzical expression
upon your face
that you're wondering
wondering why I've brought you
to this place

As I lean closer
lower my voice conspiratorially
to a whisper
I utter the words
that must change your life

'I'm giving back the monkey'
I say
and lean back
all the way now
with no obstruction

It hasn't been long
but it's been forever
that I've been carrying
this monkey for you

And it's time to return it
to its rightful owner
and guess what?
It's you!

There's a ghost that wanders through the hallways
that would echo with the sound
of footsteps
if there was anyone to hear
if there was anyone to tread those boards

Instead, that tragic figure
representative of the little deaths
accumulated over time
glides over the boards
never disturbing the dust that lies
beneath its feet

Silently peering into rooms
furnishings all covered by dust cloths
hiding the scars of being lived in
hemmed in by the gloom
that descended
ever so softly and quietly
to bury this place

Taking up the battleaxe
lying discarded in the hall
blade covered in dry, congealed blood
I start to stalk the ghost
through the void and the rooms

Swearing under my breath
as the hammering of my heart
announces its presence
– willing it to be quiet
slowing the flow of blood
through my veins
as it tries to compete

with the relentless ticking
of the old grandfather clock
in the hall
only sign now of life in this abode
good old father time
unstoppable

Whilst I seek to stalk my ghost
and lay it to its final rest

I'm an impostor
dressed in someone else's clothes
as I rifle through her wardrobe
I wonder who the hell she really was

And everyone who knew her
says they know me
and they confuse the two of us
for each other

And as soon as they open their mouths
to utter those fateful words
they condemn me to living
that girl's life

And I beat against that glass
a moth ineffectually trying
to find a way out
a way out of that room

A room that should be comforting
and familiar
but has become alien nonetheless

A life that goes on around me
whether I want it to or not
sucked into that maelstrom
drawn inexorably back into the mundane

And the bars of gold that imprison me
have lost their allure
and I can't find anyone
anyone
who seems to care
that I'm an impostor
dressed in someone else's clothes

I've lost sight of that path
I was meant to follow
it's overgrown now
with brambles and weeds
caused by my neglect

And it pricks and stings
as I try to clear the way
and set my feet upon that path
once more

Now it's a path for one
for there is no one to share
this journey with me
and I know this now

It's funny, you know
I don't remember the heart-shaped,
strawberry birthmark
or the fairy kisses on your shoulder
I never knew that you didn't like juicy fruit
and I'm sure
that there are a thousand other things
that I never knew
or forgot that I ever did
but they are irrelevant
for when I see you
again
after ten days, months or years
I know that what I will hear
will be your soul speaking to mine

There were no fireworks
no starburst of red, green and yellow
no rockets of magnificent blue
and yet love came knocking

There were animated conversations
sharing of hopes and dreams
deepening of a friendship
and still love came knocking

There was the first tender kiss
the exquisite exploring of another's body
the heights of passion
and love came knocking

There was no discussion of tomorrow
for tomorrow had no place here
and before I could open the door to love
you were gone

I will wait for you at the corner store
where we bought wizz-fizzes
and dreamt of the dawn

I will wait for you on the shore
where we danced naked
and waited for the dawn

I will wait for you in the woods
where we talked of the world
and planned for the dawn

I will wait for you on the swings
where we chased the sky
and caught the moon

I will wait for you, my love
till you shall come home again
and then we shall live for the dawn

The lock of hair tumbles on to his forehead, again. With a movement eased by long practice, he lifts his hand and pushes it back again. Again and again, this happens whilst we talk. He still wears my ring on his hand. Ring finger, right hand, snug next to that of old, polished, long-dead grandfather.

The conversation flows like silk and is awkward by turns. Like an old, battered car with an unfamiliar driver in the seat behind the wheel. It sputters into life by fits and dies again with an old man's racking cough.

There are meaningless words I can utter to fill these silences and I grasp at them. Versatile performer excelling in the art of small talk, excelling in avoiding what must be said.

Silence again. And I watch as, in crowded bar, noisy with unfamiliar strangers yet comfortable in its safety and anonymity, the Bottomless Trousers play. Discordant noise rising over the hum of lives – tales of the human situation faithfully replayed every night here. Playing at love and loss, which are only facades, always hiding that which is true – lust and power. Power to dominate and subjugate another's will. Make them into your puppet. Turn them into the ideal. Then stand back with critical eye. Artist appraising completed masterpiece. Eyeing each detailed brushstroke. Pondering the finished work. Strangely dissatisfying now. The ideal to which one was attracted cannot maintain and sustain life once it has been seen by trick of light in another, then made real. Accusation bursting forth from tongue but ready to explode, bitten back in frustration and anger. Question in eyes, heart and mind. You've changed, you're not the ideal I fell in love with, made you into. I never had room for you in the ideal and I still haven't figured out my mistake.

Noise fading, overwhelmed by voices, only to rise discordant once more in dingy and crowded meat marketplace. How much for your flesh, good lady? I just want a taste, a sample. I have all these things to offer. But I am only transitory, transient. Surely you knew that all along?

I watch as you gaze at the place on the wall, covered with advertisements and memory by turn, that has compelled you all evening. Your gaze always returning there, your mind elsewhere, somewhere I'll never be able to reach. The gaze returns to capture mine for an instant.

'I heard you were on the prowl,' I hear you ask. You wait for the answer and hope flares anew. Foolish hope – hard to quench and destroy. In a parallel universe which I seem to be existing in – not the one I have desired and imagined – I hear myself reply. I'm available but not looking. In spite of my betrayals, I have always been true to you. An honesty, I am to discover, that you do not deserve and have never deserved. Not in this universe, perhaps, but a parallel one. Ideals are such powerful things and the die was cast for this honesty, long ago, when I shed all my armour for you. For you to stab, poke and torture the fleshy bits. Strangely, I recall an old teacher of English saying, 'Always keep some secrets. Retain a sense of mystery and retain, contain, the man.'

What I want to say, but do not have the courage yet, is how can I be so when you broke my heart? Demolished the ideal. Silence falls in this space between you and me again.

The dilapidated wreck sputters into life once more. Conversation more animated now. Beer warming my belly. And always I watch you. Watch the achingly familiar mannerisms. Glancing at the hands that roamed once over my body in your first voyage of discovery. Looking at your mouth as you speak, remembering the taste of you, the feel of your tongue dancing with mine. The shock of remembered desire, buried for so long, warming me once more. Hope lurking at my shoulder now, peering at you with myopic eyes. Whispering in my ear, 'He still wants you. He will be all you imagined and more. He will return to you. It's your turn tonight.'

The last silence falls for the evening. Softly enveloping. I will count to ten, I tell myself, and then speak. One, two…ten. Deep breath, straighten backbone, gather courage, launch the ship. Remember when you asked if we were okay? I've done it now, coldly impersonal and I listen to you speak. Now, phrases stand out. He has absolved himself of guilt and yet both are guilty here, trying to ignore blood-stained hands. Forgive me father, for I have sinned. Please allow me to dodge retribution and forgive me my trespasses.

It was a mistake. I think that is the phrase from this tortured conversation that shall stay with, haunt, me. I've given him back the monkey but it is not enough. I want to hurt him. Not callously, or through deceit, but I want him to get out of his head and see another's pain through those eyes of a dreamer, focused ever inward.

'Cunt, asshole, bastard, prick,' I want to scream. But they were never my style, will never pierce the veneer. And so I reclaim my tightly controlled self and allow myself to cry. Building it up. Despairing of the ideal. Despairing of ever being loved as I know you could love me if you would. If you grew up and cast aside your ideals. Playthings I discarded long ago. Soul mate, once I called you. Still true now, you have what I desire; but petty, mean spirit will not share it.

You take my cold hand in yours, uncomfortable now. And when I openly weep, take me into your arms and hold me. I've closed the door now; I gave back the monkey and I've denied you the friendship you need and crave. Not good karma but, needs must, I look out for Number One now. So very glad I do not have your karma.

And I leave the bar called the Phoenix, and you, behind. Good name for a bar and the playing of this last act in the play that you and I wrote together.

The jester sits
　　cap awry
nonchalantly swinging his feet
tapping against Jack (in the box)
out of time with the tinkle
of bells from his head
– the cap that is
for he is not yet insane

All around him are coins
some this way
some that
for while chaotic patterns are unpredictable
they are not random

Nor is the death
that our jester is trying decide
if he would like to try it
feeling jaded and malcontented with life
he thinks to choose between life and death

For he is the Jester
and he is the fool
– man, that is

'What maketh the man?' the famous man once asked
(for women had no place in his world)
Is it possible to distil the essences
of a person's life
– their soul –
pour them into a jar
labelled

Enter the babe
newborn
'mewling and puking'
demanding

Watch the babe grow
into an adult
observe the influences
an anonymous scribe
noting
a word, a glance, a gesture, a touch

With objectivity
works the nameless scribe
or so they think

For what is the scribe
but memory
remembering the hurt, the pain, the rejection
huddling in a foetal position
in the deepest recesses of the mind

Lurking
behind that corner
the love's eyes
the mother's love
the father's dreams

Waiting to strike
unleashing
primal scream
anguish

Relentless
reminding
constantly
of failure

Failure of memory
which seeks to confuse
the reality and the dream

And so we ask
the immortal
timeless
question

What maketh the man?

And we delve into memory of a man
for each
is different
thus the essence
for each
must be distilled with care
so as not to lose a precious drop
of the life essence

Seeking the scribblings of the anonymous scribe
stored in the vaults of memory
tainted by time

To continue forth in this fashion
is to store
row upon row
of bottles
of the sweetest fragrance
known to humankind
the essence of one

Thus we can gather bottles
of this fragrance
selecting those
with the sweetest fragrance
to savour

And by prophesying backwards
may receive a glimpse
of a soul
that hurts with the brightest light
of untarnished joy

However,
in selecting the sweetest fragrances
we play tricks
upon ourselves
as surely
as memory does

For we are all entwined
in this life
as the butterfly in South America
surely knows

And we must savour
the sweetest fragrance
with the sour
to observe the truth

But what of truth?
objective?
different cultures and points of view
will disagree
and I now
and I then
will surely disagree
as to what truth is, was

Thus we shall journey
watch the players
enact
their precious and trivial lives
with our imperfect scribes
recording a word, a glance, a gesture, a touch

At the end we shall
disagree about the truth
with each
seeing
what they wish
– what their essences have shaped them
to perceive

And for a brief
elusive
moment
their lives will have touched
and then

nothing

For it is not
in our nature
to share our hopes and dreams,
with fears
we will not even admit
to our innermost soul

On West 46 and Broadway
there's newly martyred Christians
selling salvation
whilst kitty-cornered across the road
the devil sells damnation
for only the price of your soul

And it's kinda weird
how there's always a crowd
around Beelzebub's limo
whilst people avoid the gazes
of God's honest foot soldiers

Revolting, repugnant, repulsive
reeking of stale urine

Filthy, furtive, frightened
matted hair covering
evasive, violated, abused eyes
far older than the accompanying countenance

Quick-bitten fingers
grime engrained under the nails
hands sullied by filth and pain
outstretched as
panhandling on street corner
multiple layers of clothing
all her worldly goods and chattels
in the forty-degree heat

Don't touch, see, hear, smell or feel her
poverty may not be contagious
but fear is

Zombie turned square-eyes
numbing synapses of brain
eyelids sewn open
slack-jawed
drool making snail trails
towards weak chin

Constant diet of violence
screening every night
red blood looking fake
as ketchup never does
agony over in a minute
eating sound bites of violence
for dinner

Tonight's meal, dear
will be
desensitisation of death

As a woman I am privileged
to bleed once a month
and for the shedding of my womb
I must pay a luxury tax on tampons
and I can no longer use PMS as an excuse for murder
but sheer murder it is

As a woman I am privileged
to be independent
I can earn the same wage as a man
and yet I have to deal everyday in the workplace
with the old boys' network
As a woman I can live alone or with friends
in this patriarchal society
with the freedom of choice, voice and mind
and yet I cannot walk the streets alone without fear
my keys between my fingers to ward off evil

As a woman I am privileged
to receive the same education as men
and yet in the classroom the larrikin, the nerd, the booner
– the boys – are the apples of the teacher's eye
and I just a girl to be ignored, subdued
CONSTRAINED

As a woman I am privileged
to be able to express my emotions
– well, not all of them, because anger
glorious, empowering, freeing
ANGER
remains a taboo

Gaunt human skeleton
skin stretched grotesquely over protruding bones
sunken eyes smudged with grey
lit by a fanatical light
covered, by day, by loose baggy clothes
at night, examined every inch
in front of mirror in harsh light distorting
tricking the mind's eye
pulling handfuls of skin
fretting over weight that still won't go

Exertion, exercise, emancipation
freeing the soul from the constraints of the body
delaying menstruation
denying womanhood
succumbing to society's ideals of beauty
only skin deep here
thank God, not flesh deep
for there's barely enough of that to go around

Bloodied hands ripping out
unborn foetuses
in the name of freedom of choice

Bloodied hands murdering
the guilty
in the outrage of loss of unborn life

Balancing the scales
meting out justice
placing on one half
your sins
always keeping mine hidden

Hair flaming amazement
screaming, 'look at me'
earnest, eager tone of voice
grating on ears with
honeyed insincerities
pointed, barbed comments
disguised beneath veneer of apology

Practising sycophant
singling out men
whose feet to worship at
guru on a pedestal
self-abasement on a stick
no shame or sense of pride here

Professional women
two-piece business suits
pseudo-men
no shoulder pads here

Sorry love, you've got no balls
so you can't be one of the guys
can't be promoted
you'll be going on maternity leave
don't you know?
I'm sure you can understand
my position

Vitriolic, vicious stream of abuse
spawned, spewing forth
from a carnelian-ringed void

Eyes too small, too close together
narrowed in hostility and hate
burning into the back of his head

Vermilion talons
filed to razor-sharp points
tapping impatiently, angrily
against the laminated table top

Honeyed nectar
dripping from his tongue
soothing and placating
the tidal wave of her abuse

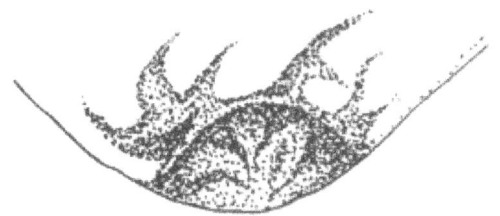

Fanatical, twisted mind
distorting, giving lie to the facts
plunging me into
the depths of despair
cleverly manipulating
feelings and emotions
playing fuck-mind games
controlling the puppet on a string

But oh!
she plays the victim so well
knows all of her lines by heart
consummate at setting the stage
lulling in new players
props, ready to hand
discarding those who have had
the silken bonds broken
the veil lifted from their eyes
this predatory vampire
feeding on human misery and despair

Primitive, rhythmic, orgasmic
relentless pounding beat of drums
hypnotising, lulling into trance-like state
frenetic, frantic gyrations of body
glowing with sweat pouring from pores
worshipping the music and its creator
lines of faithful, diligently facing demigod
minds subsumed into an enormous whole
eyes glazed from sweet chemical oblivion

Peaking, peaking
oh my God!
ecstasy,
as
mind blown away
on a chemical high
coming down now
a lover leaving for the night
please don't go
please

Yet still I live
though wax moons shine
and shed tears of blood
causing the shadow of the goddess
to fall like rain
upon my face

The primal chant wells in my soul
the symphony rising
in my drumming blood
her language coming unbidden
to the tongue
the essential worship beginning now

www.ingramcontent.com/pod-product-compliance
Lightning Source LLC
Chambersburg PA
CBHW071039080526
44587CB00015B/2693